This is dedicated to
the many inspiring
people who have decorated
my life with all the spices
of love ~ I am in awe.

Scott

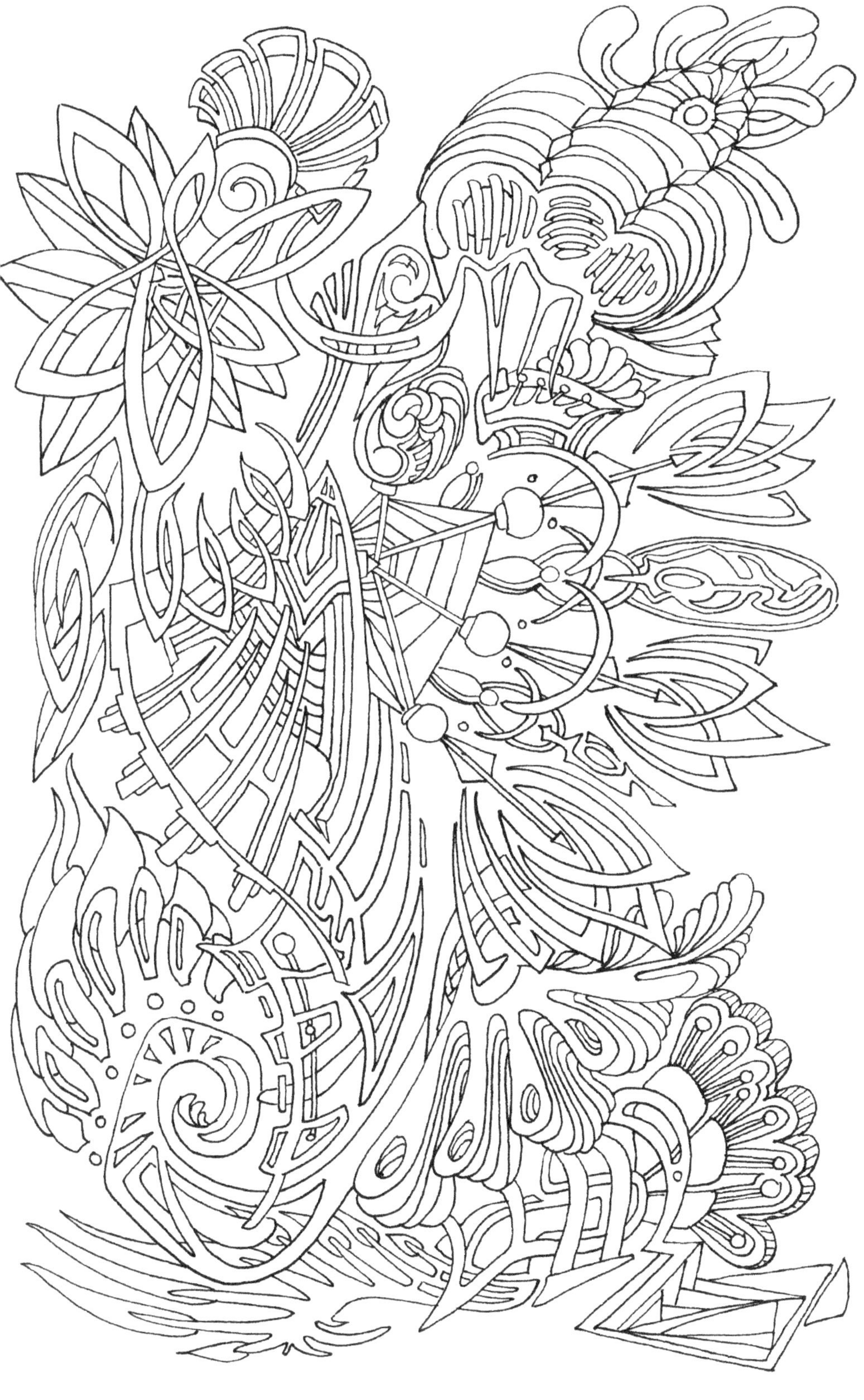

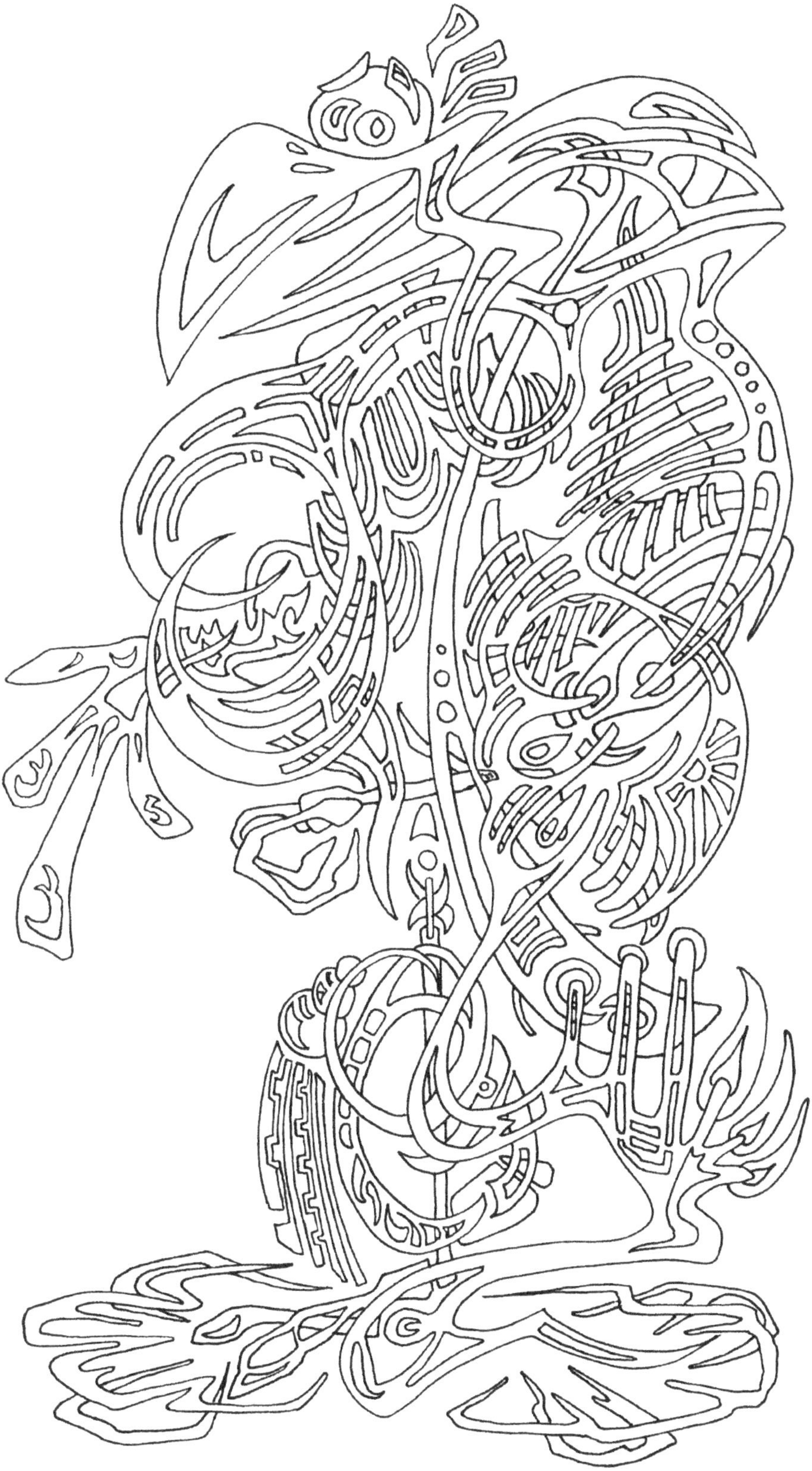

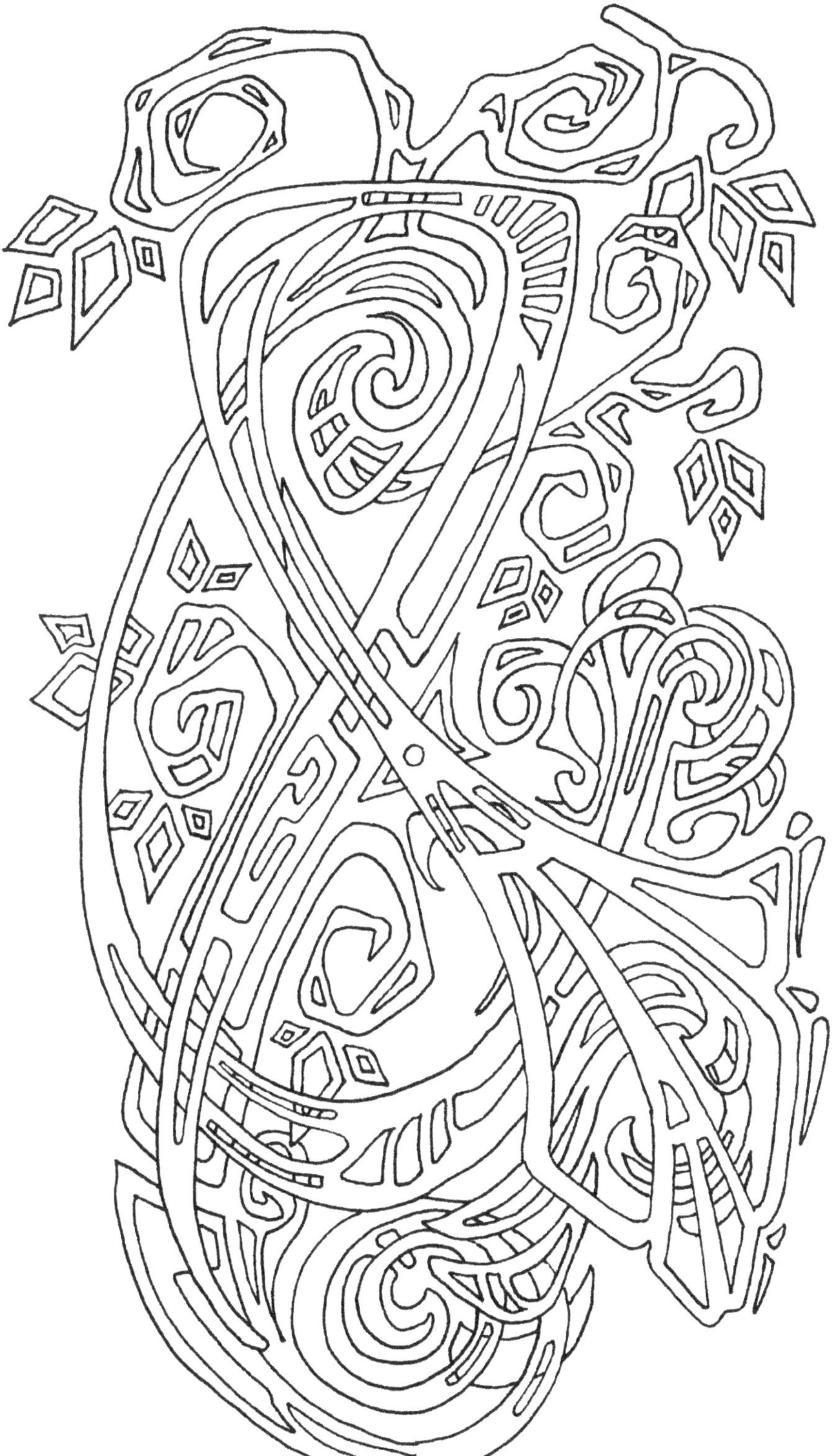

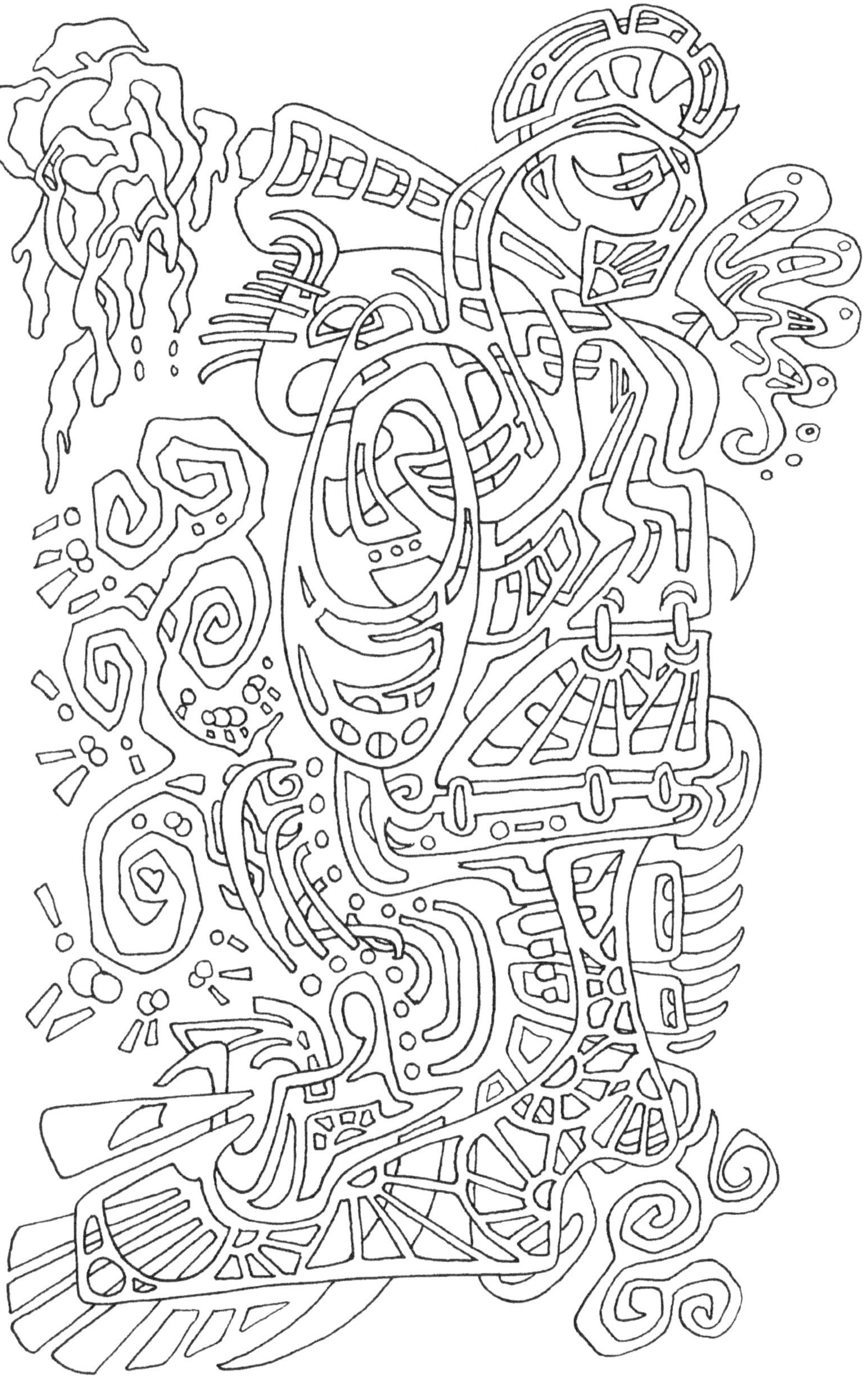

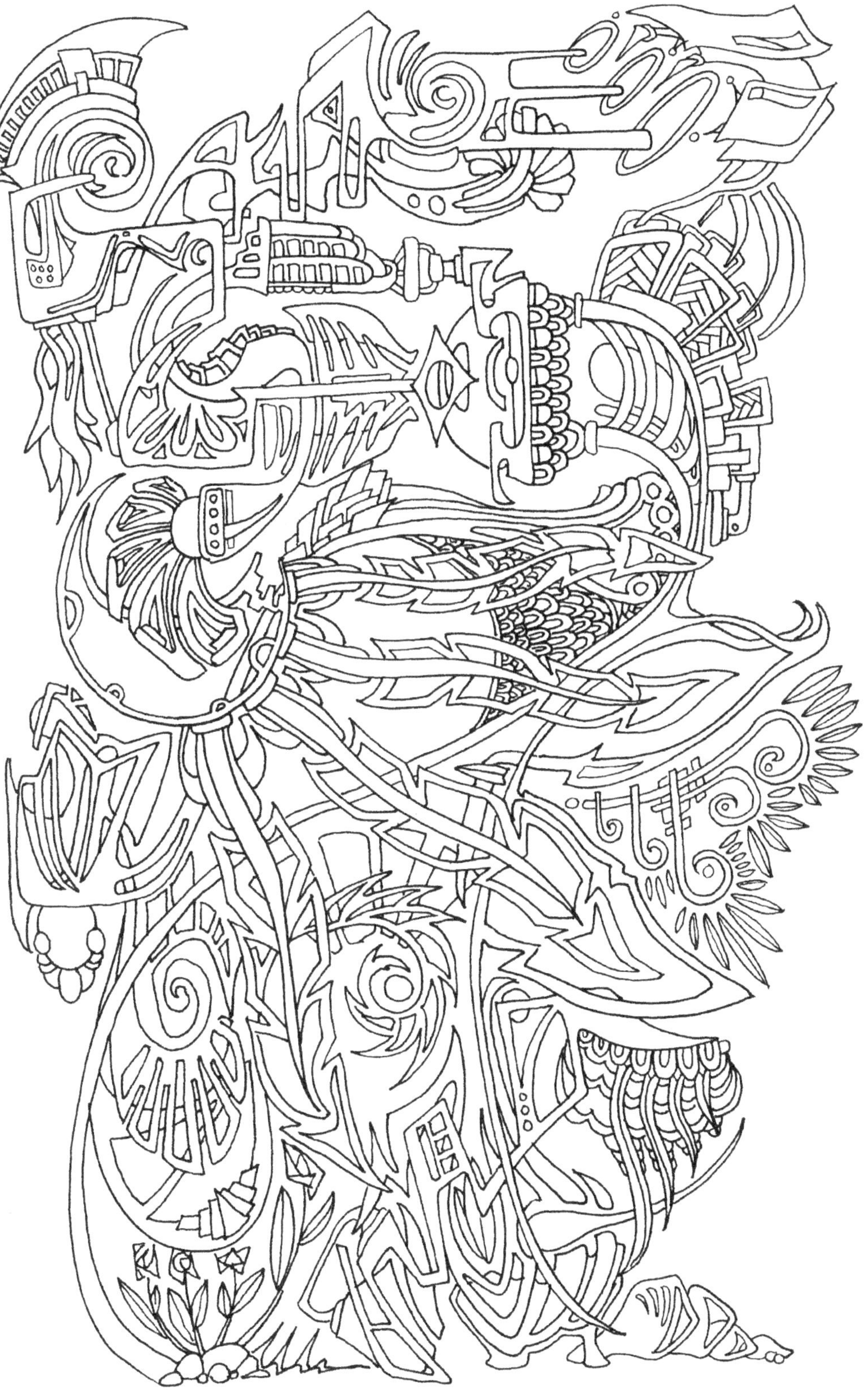

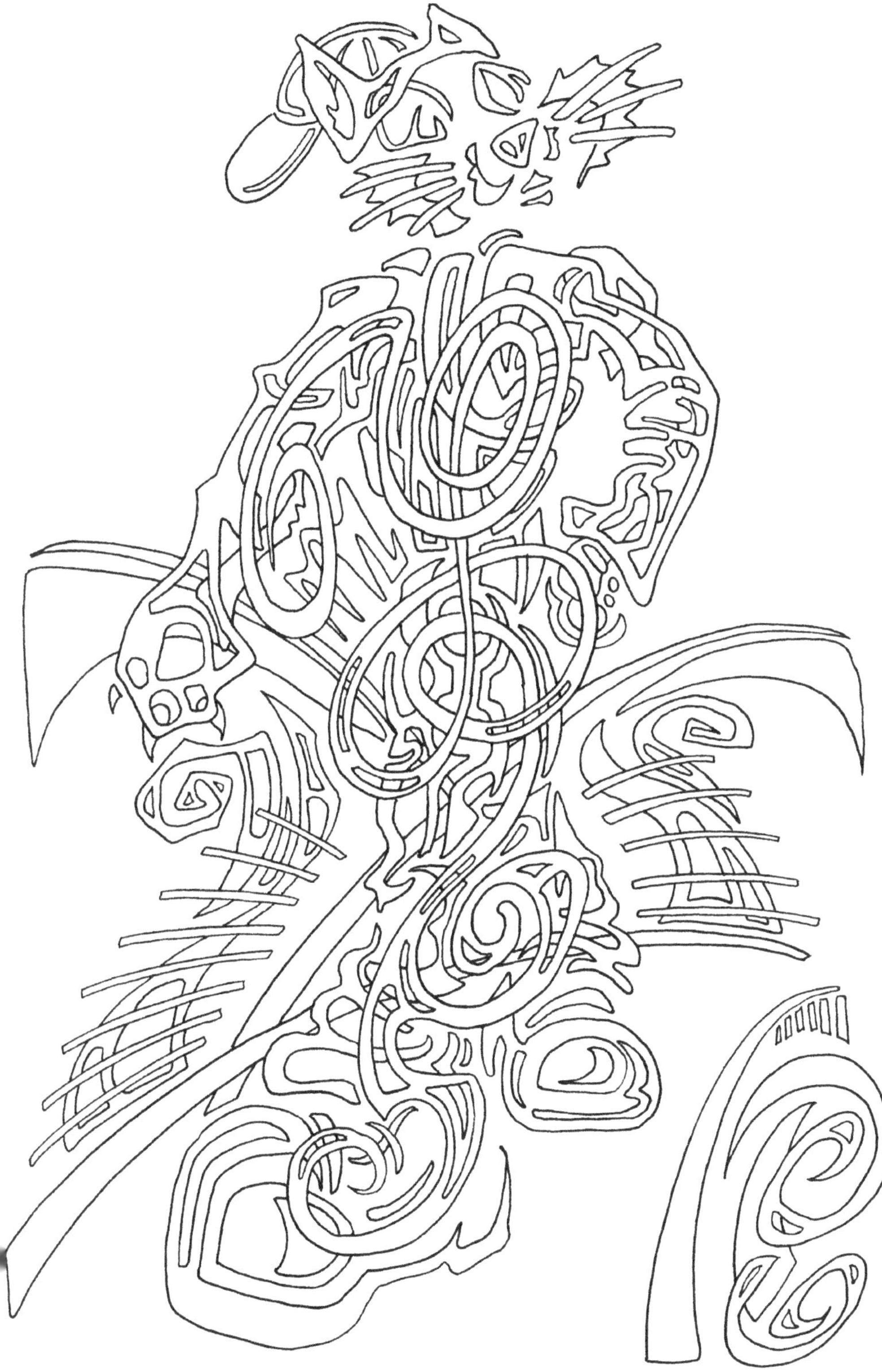

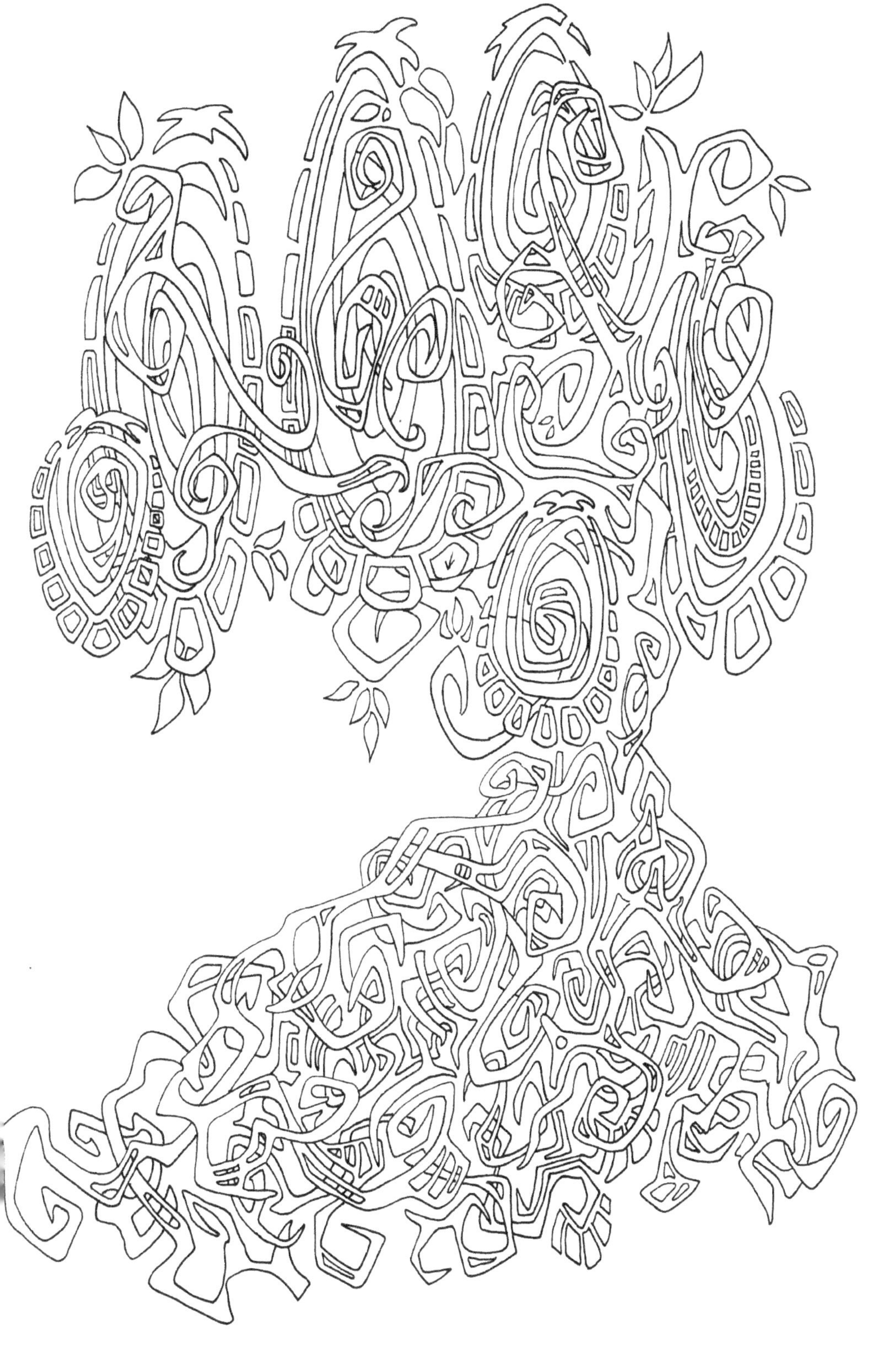

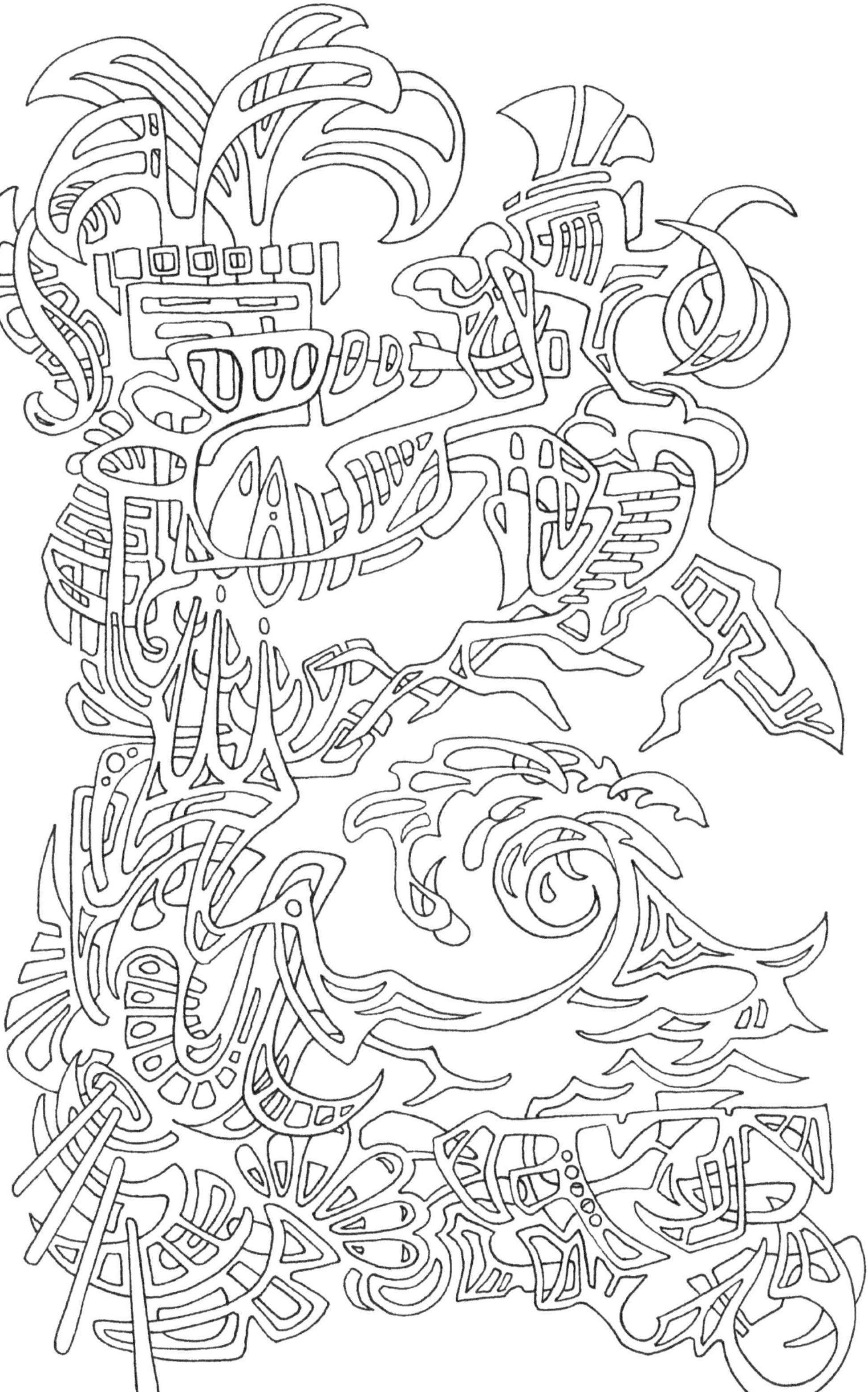

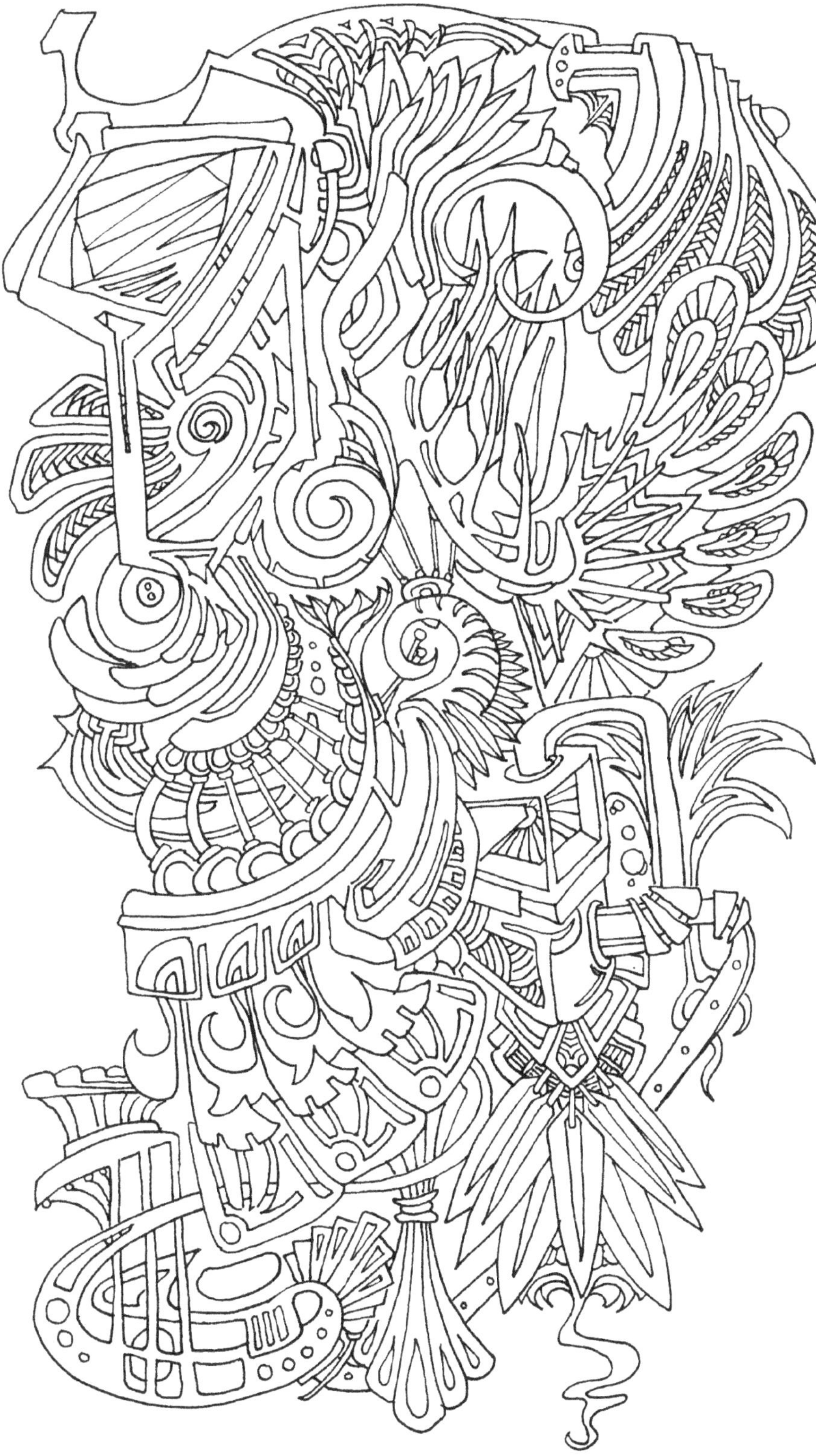

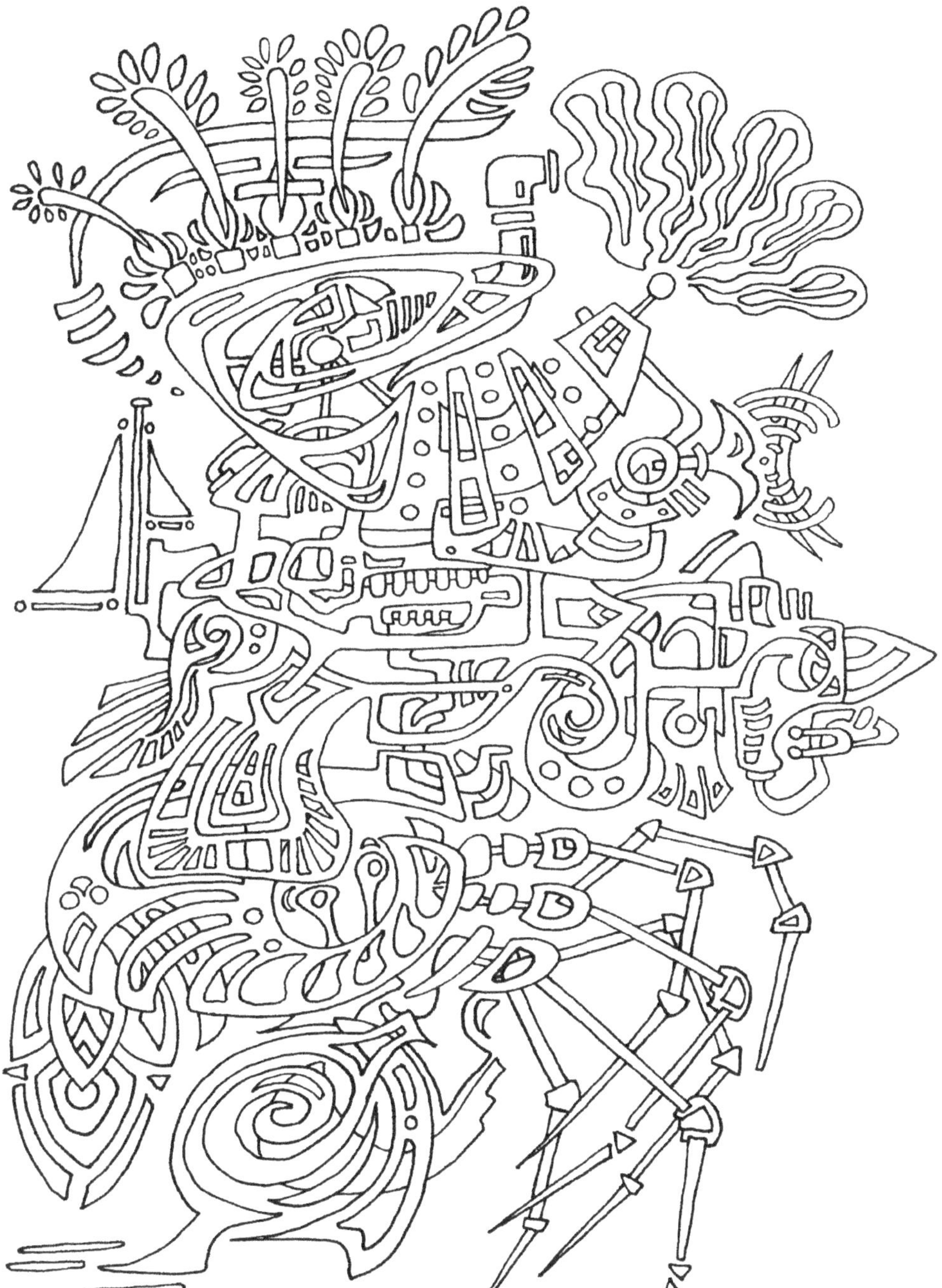

Snail Armada

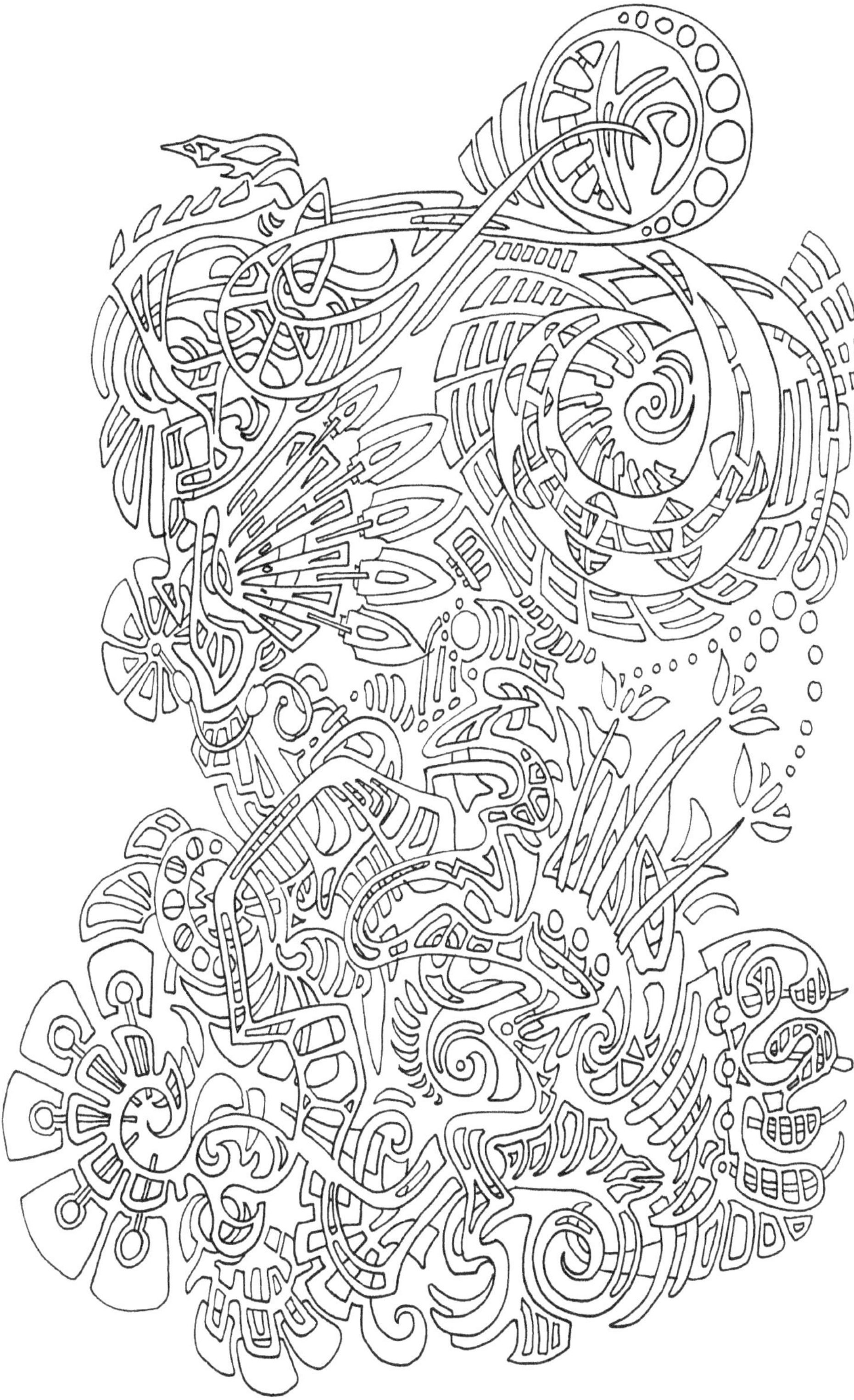

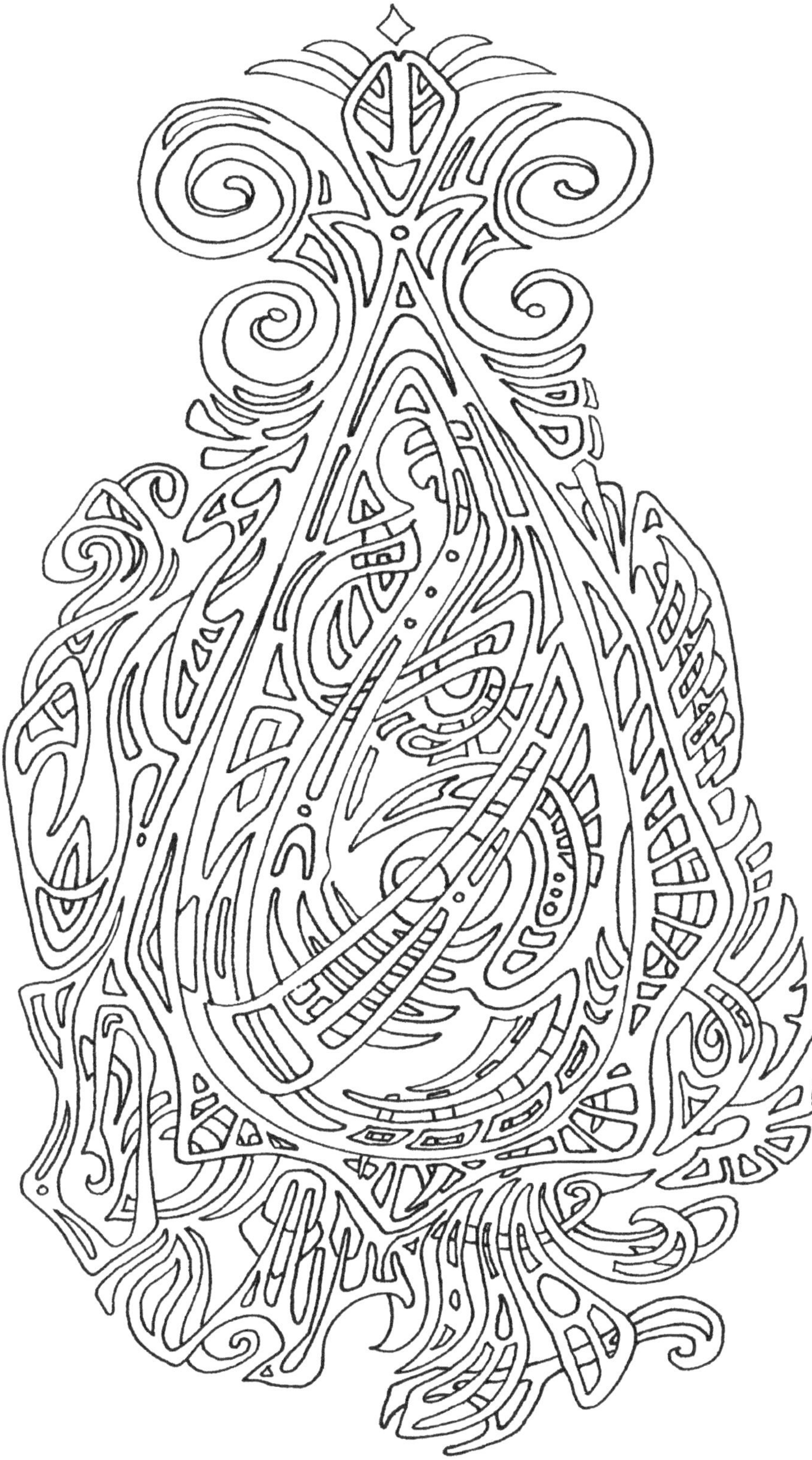

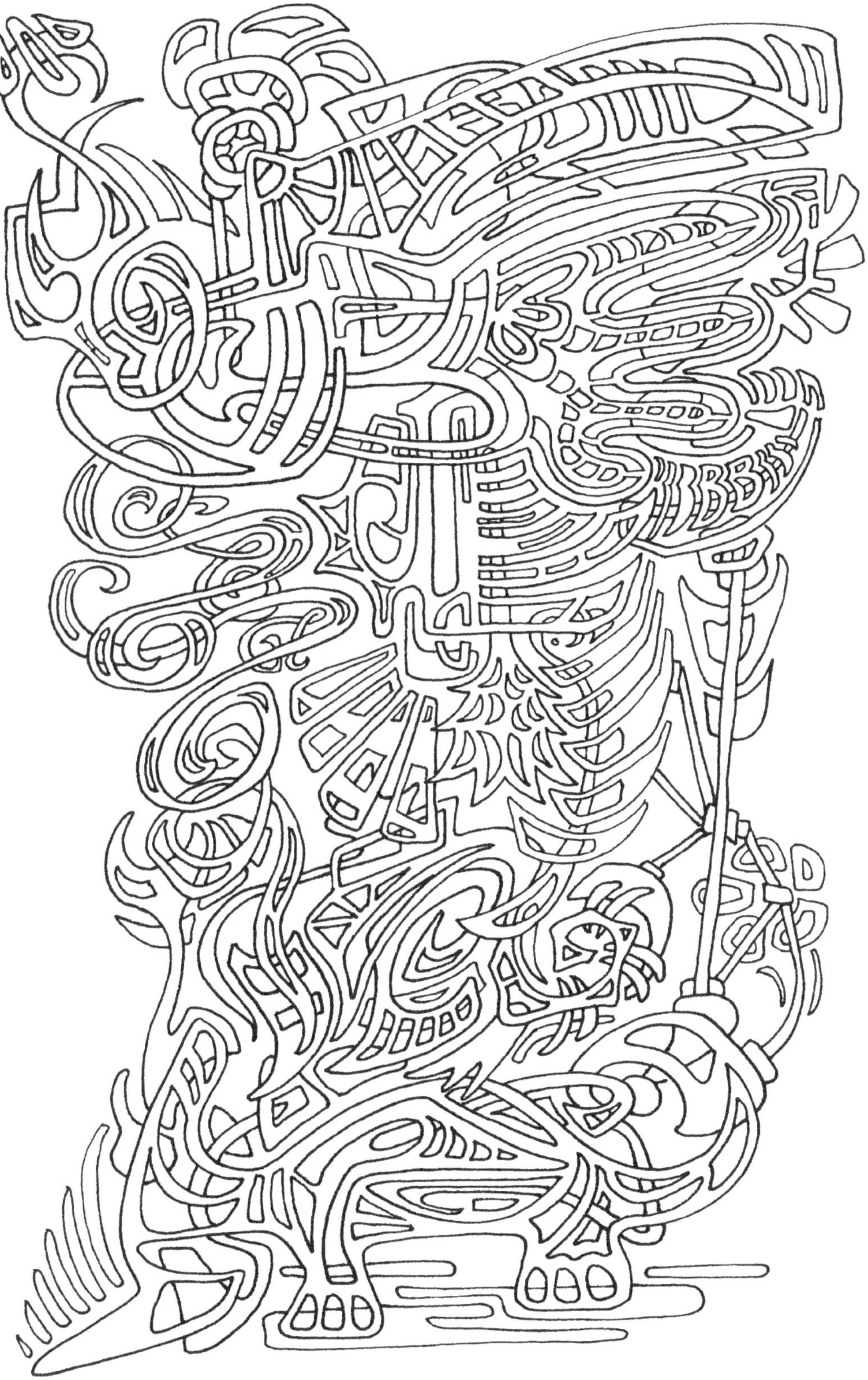

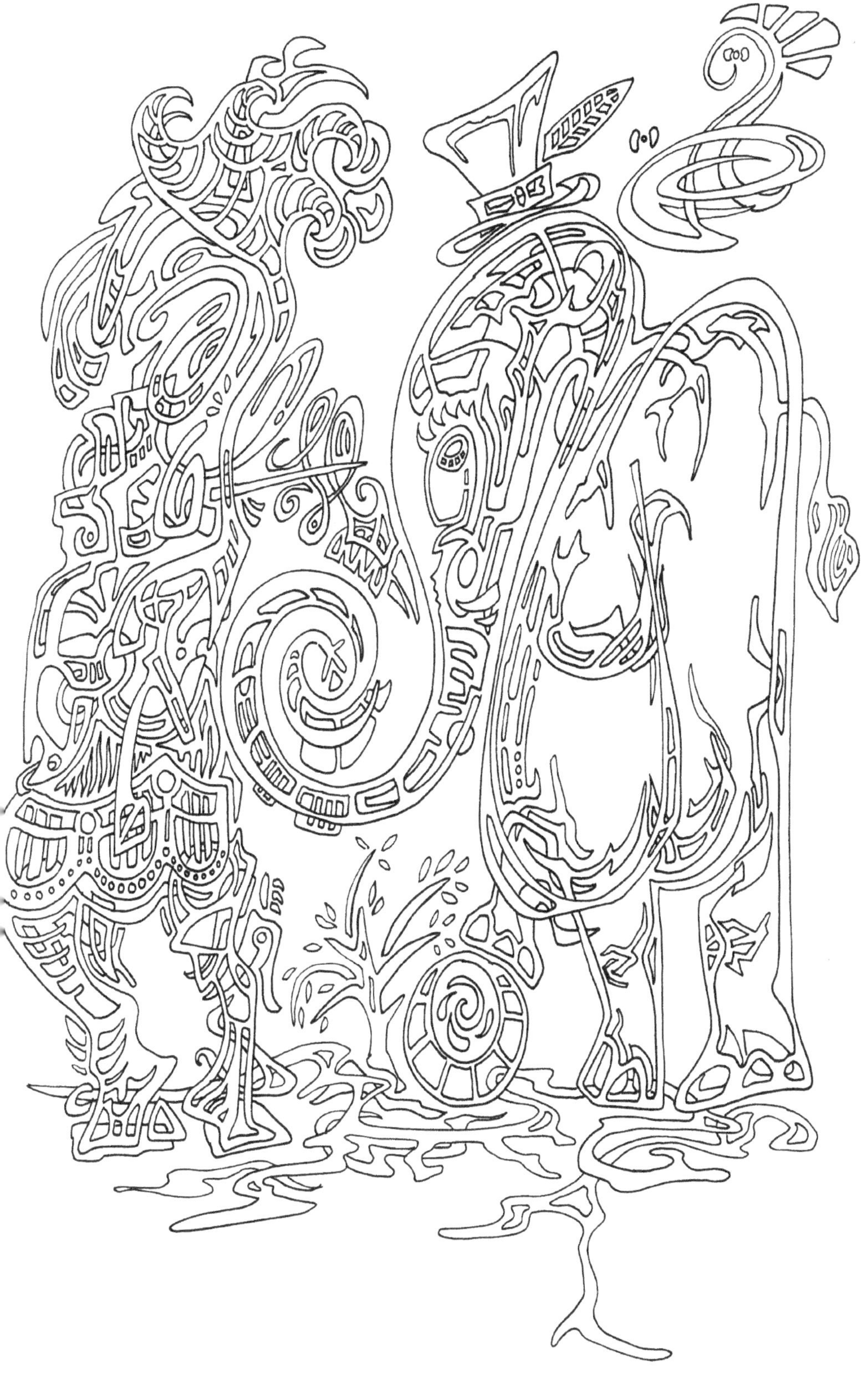

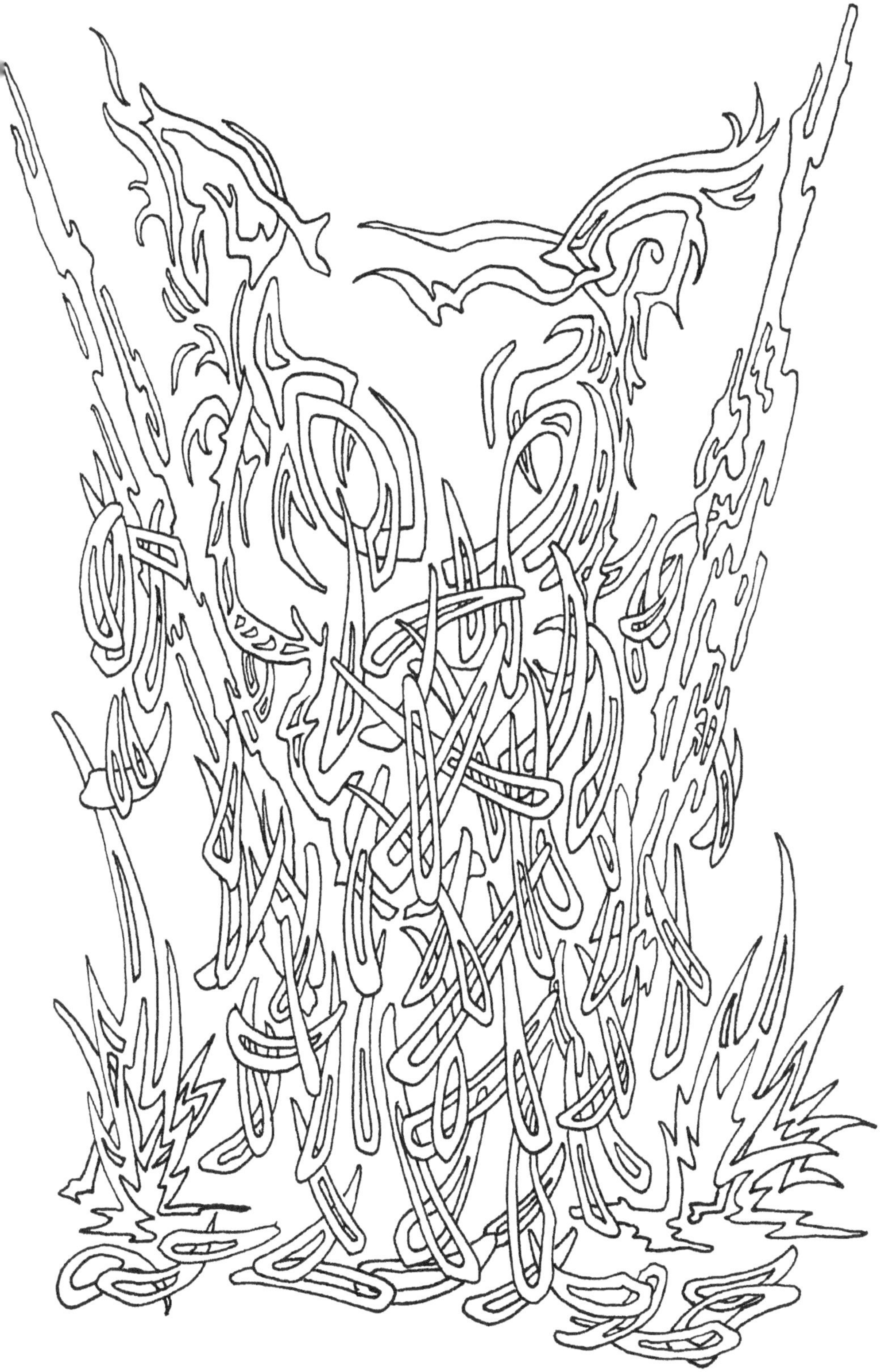

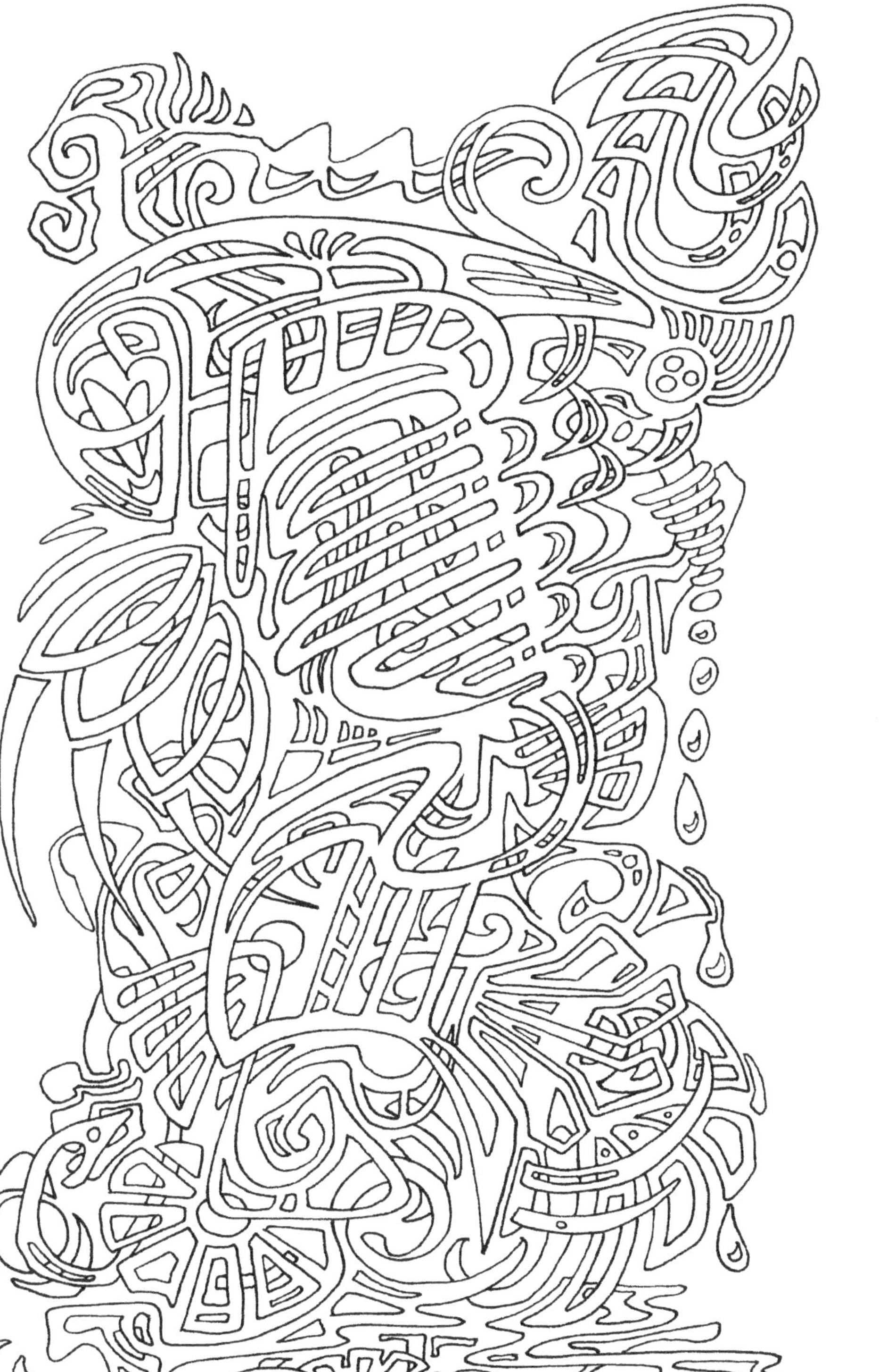

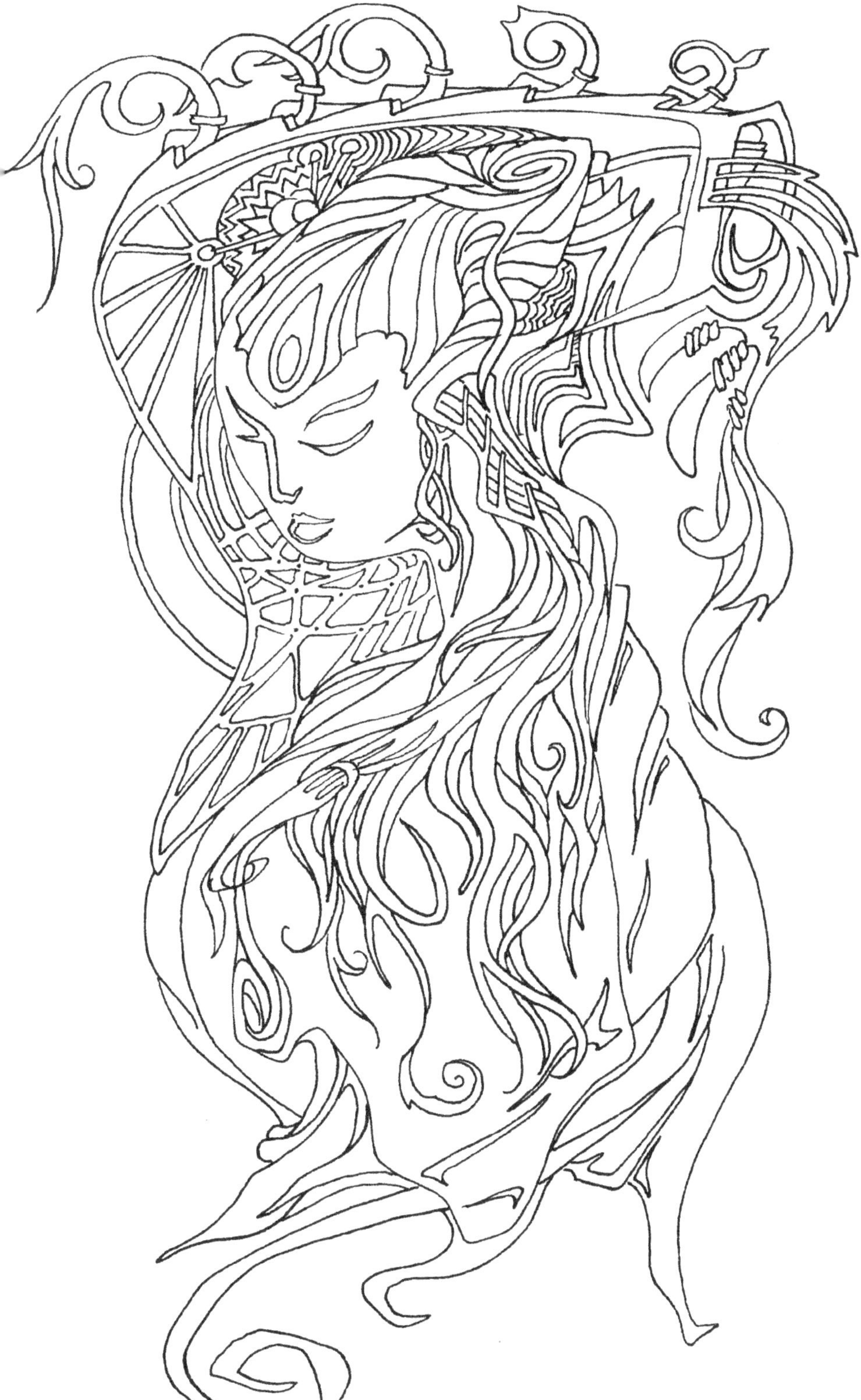

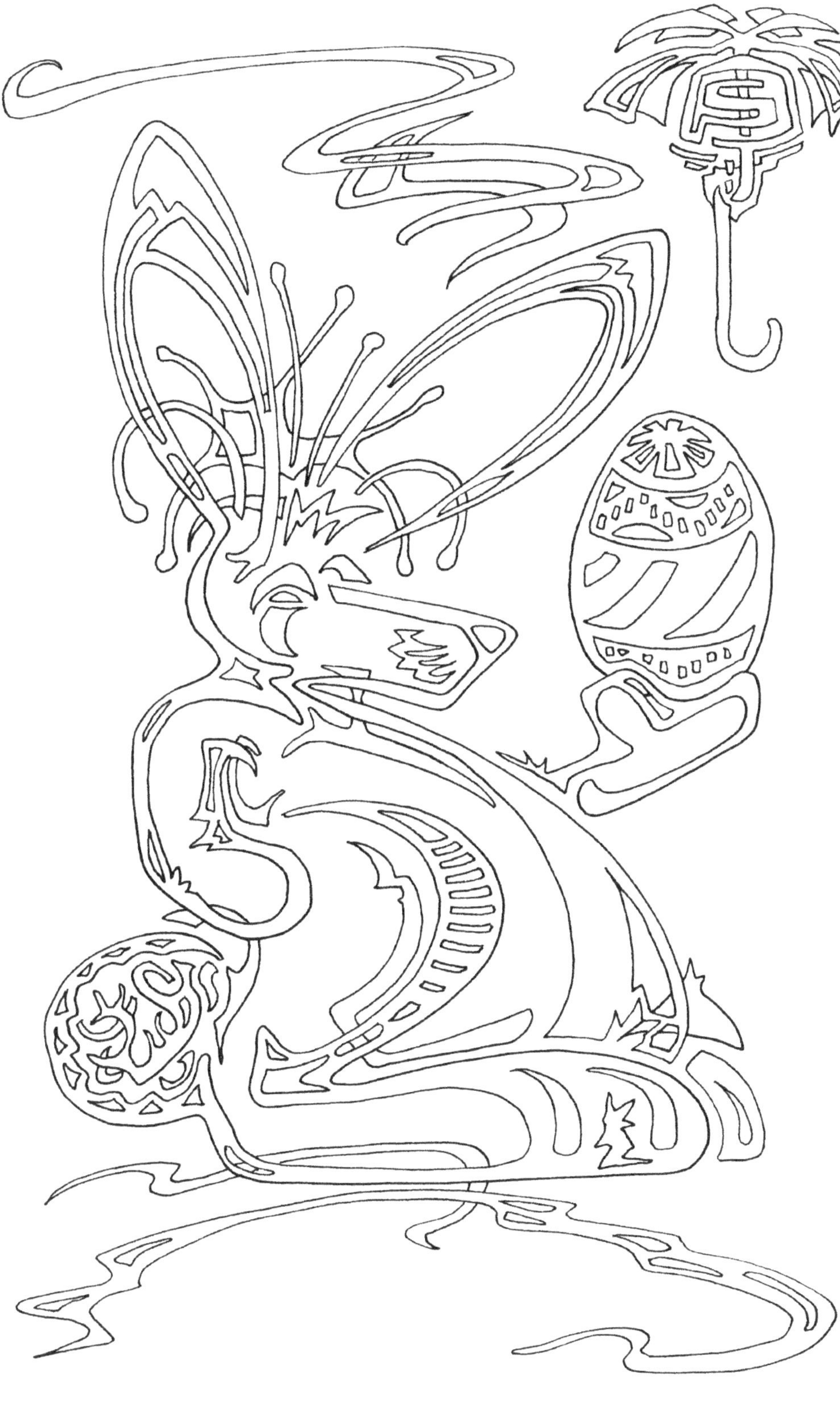

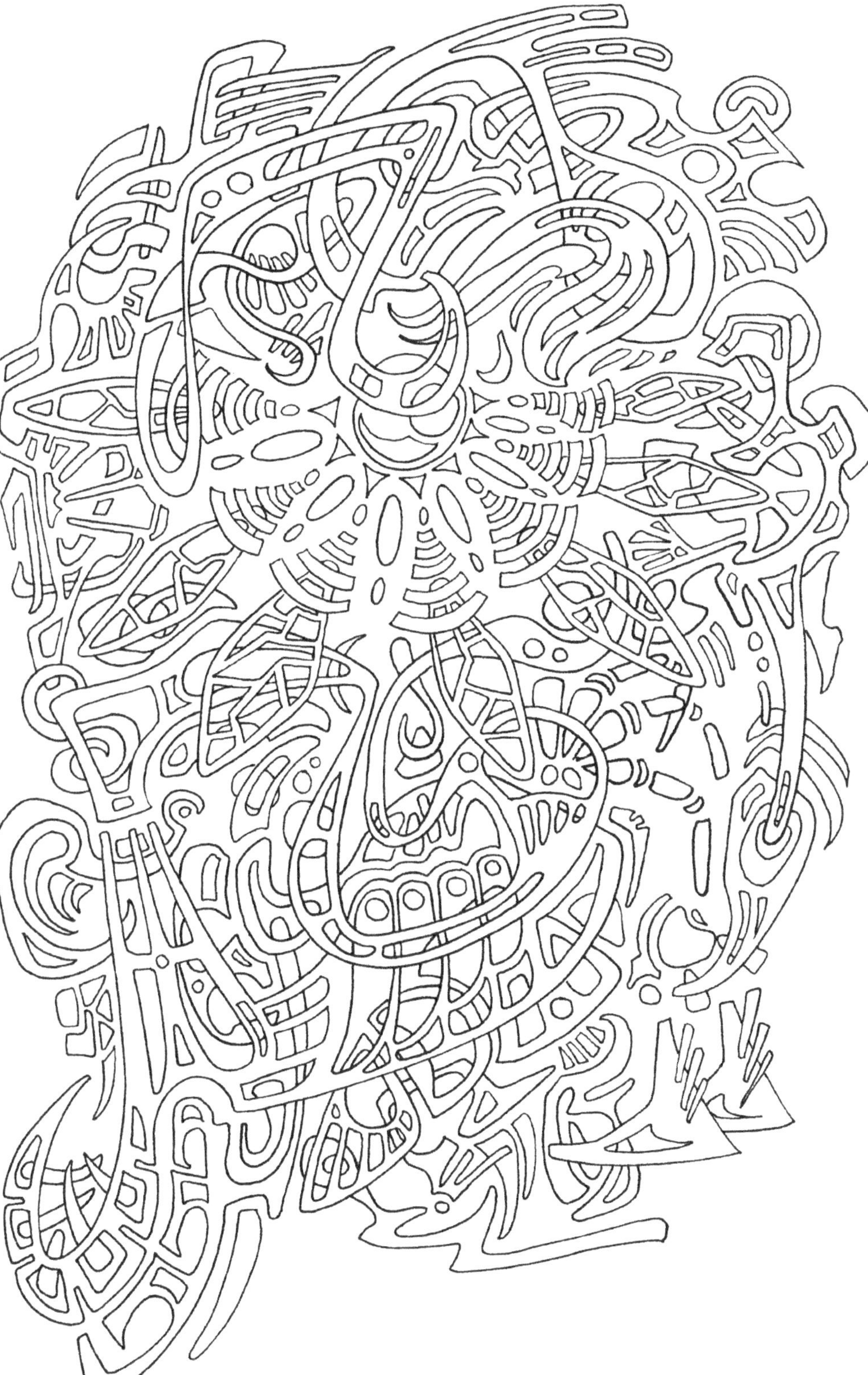

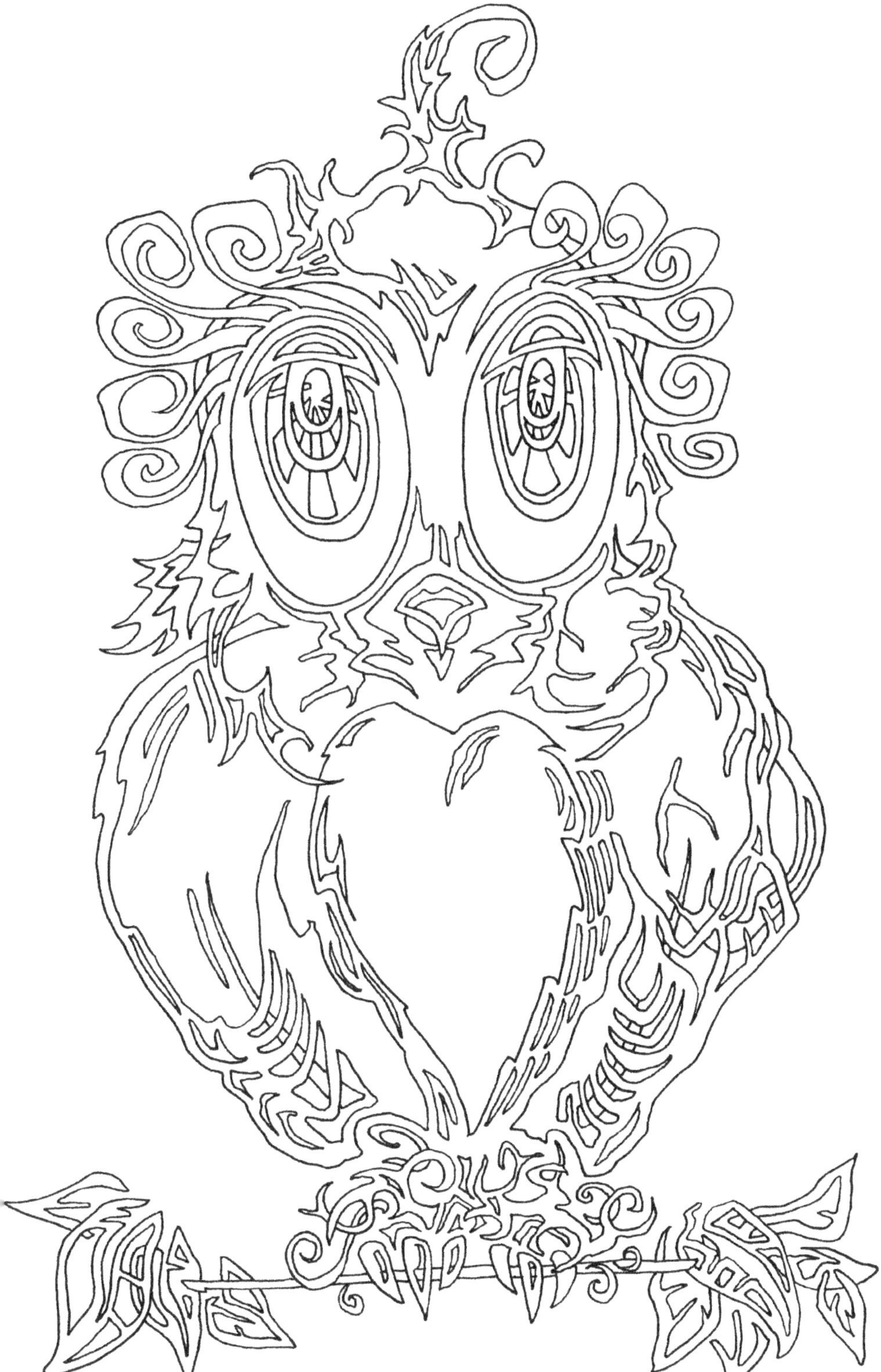

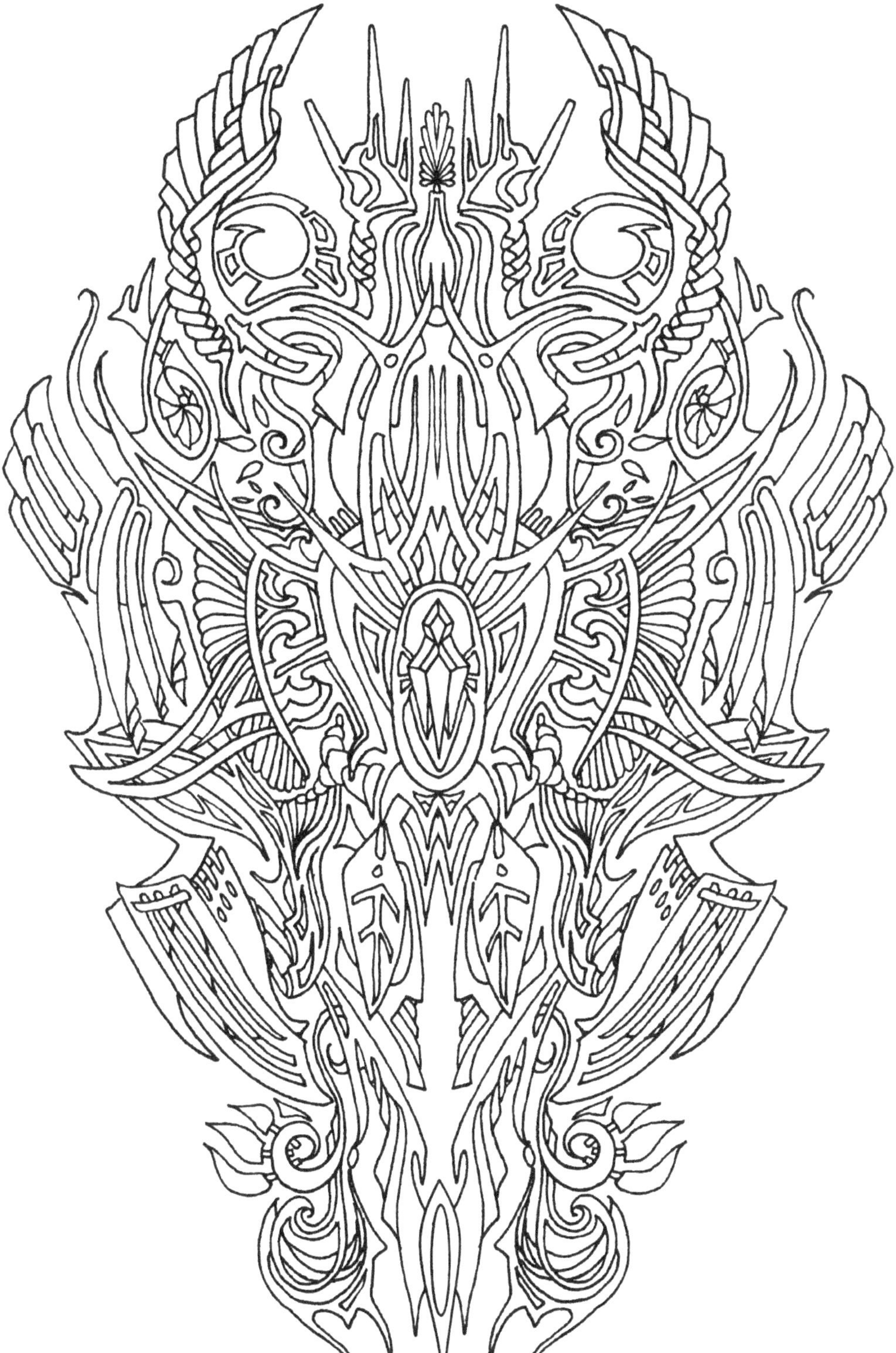

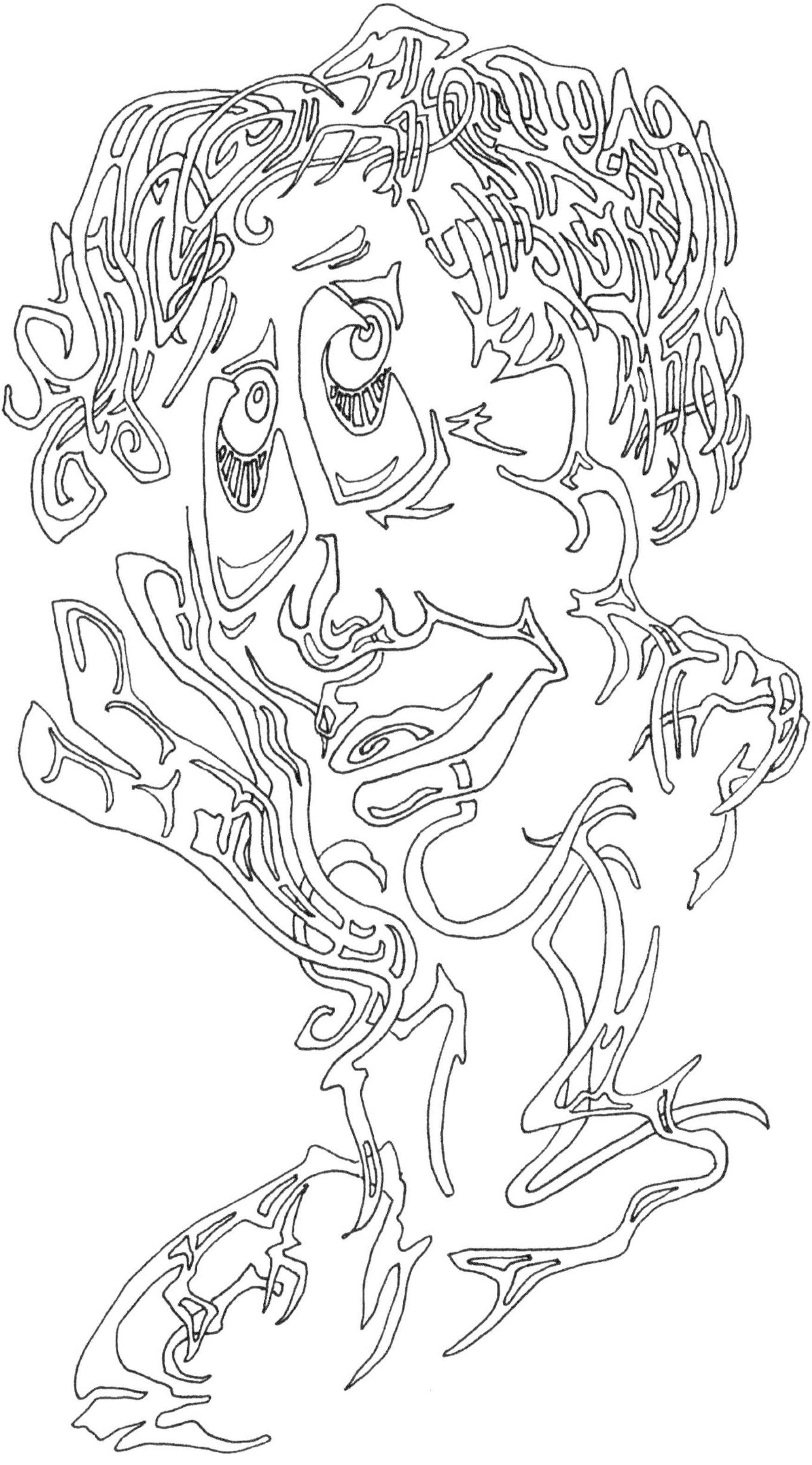

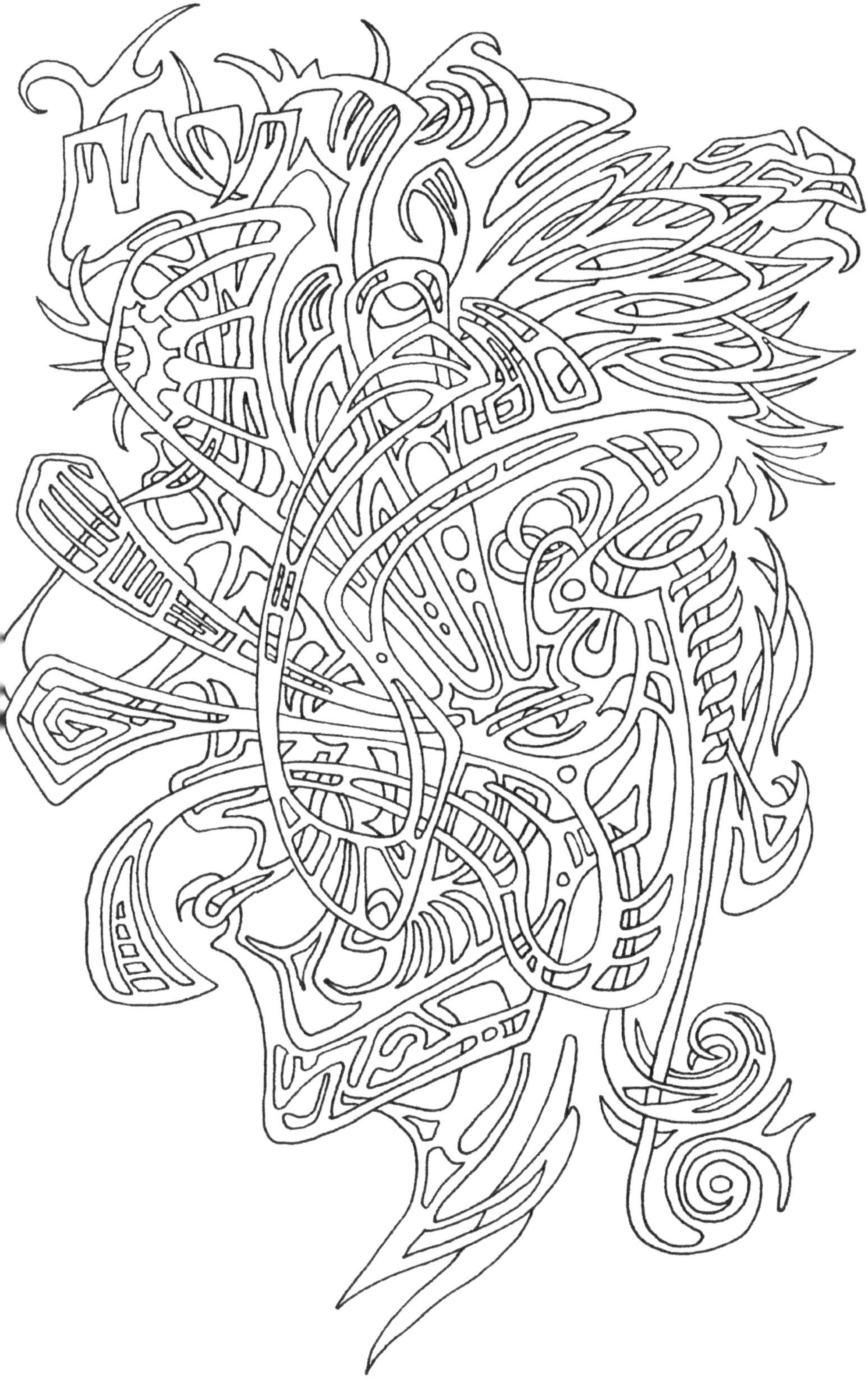

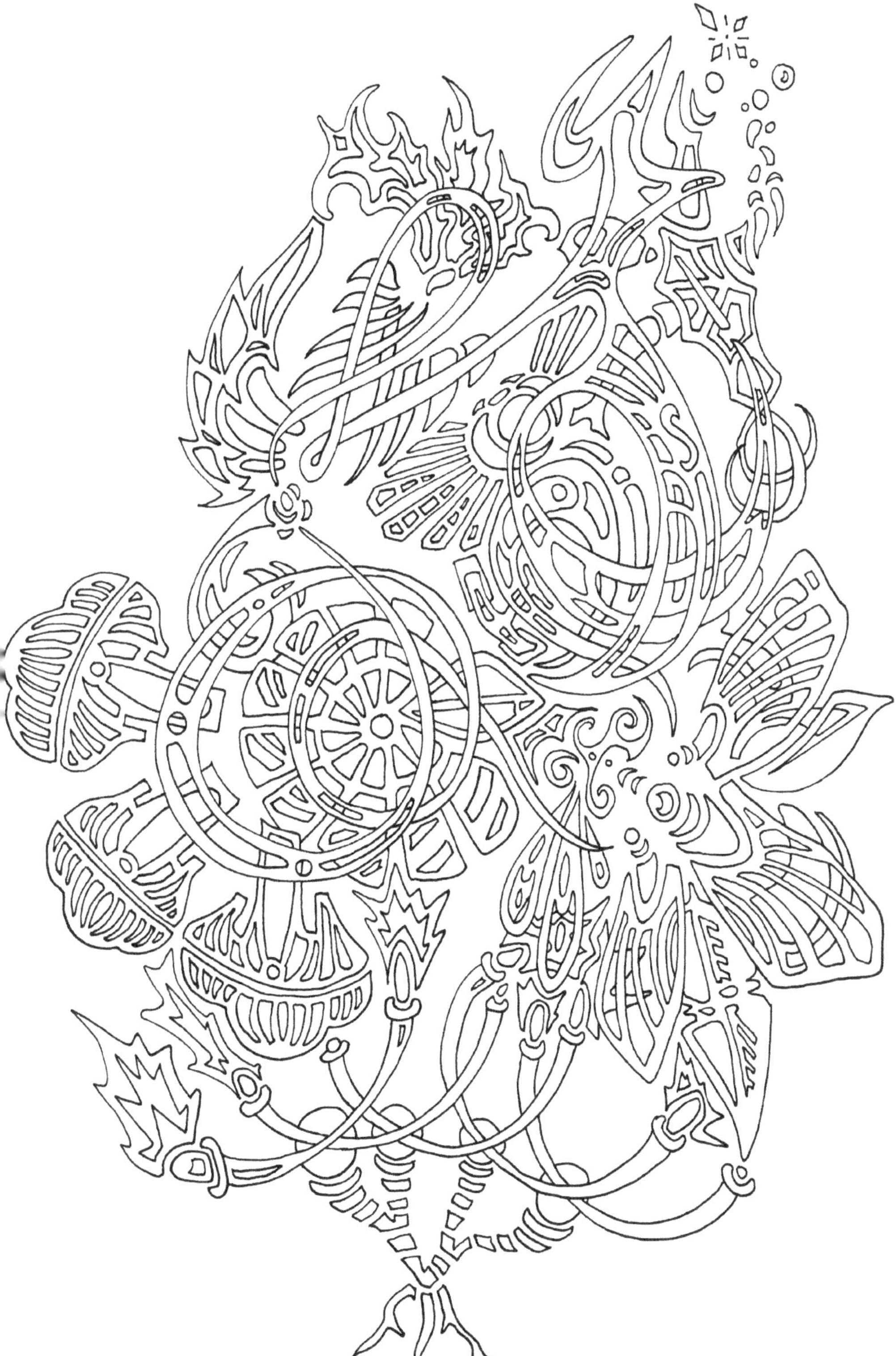

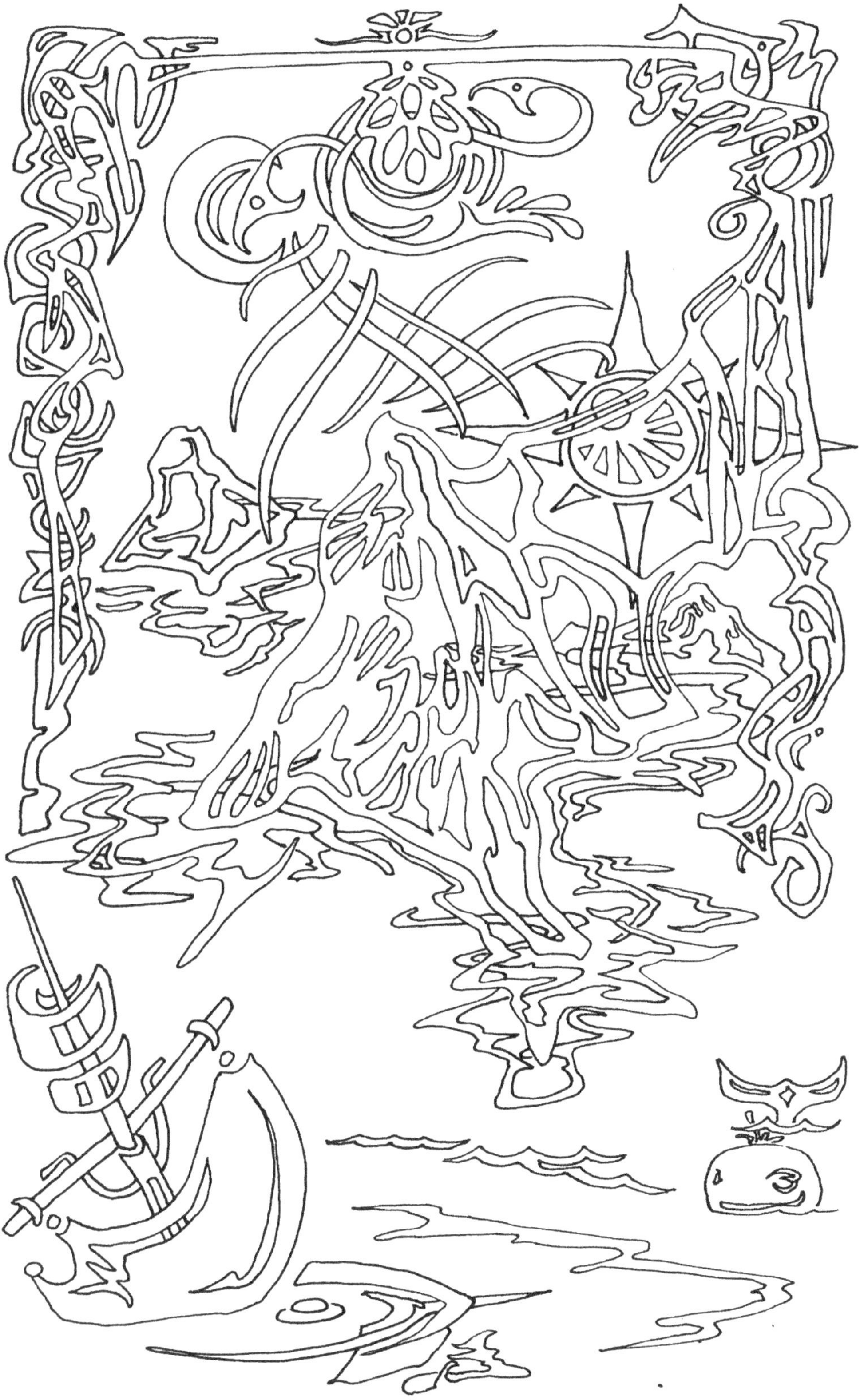

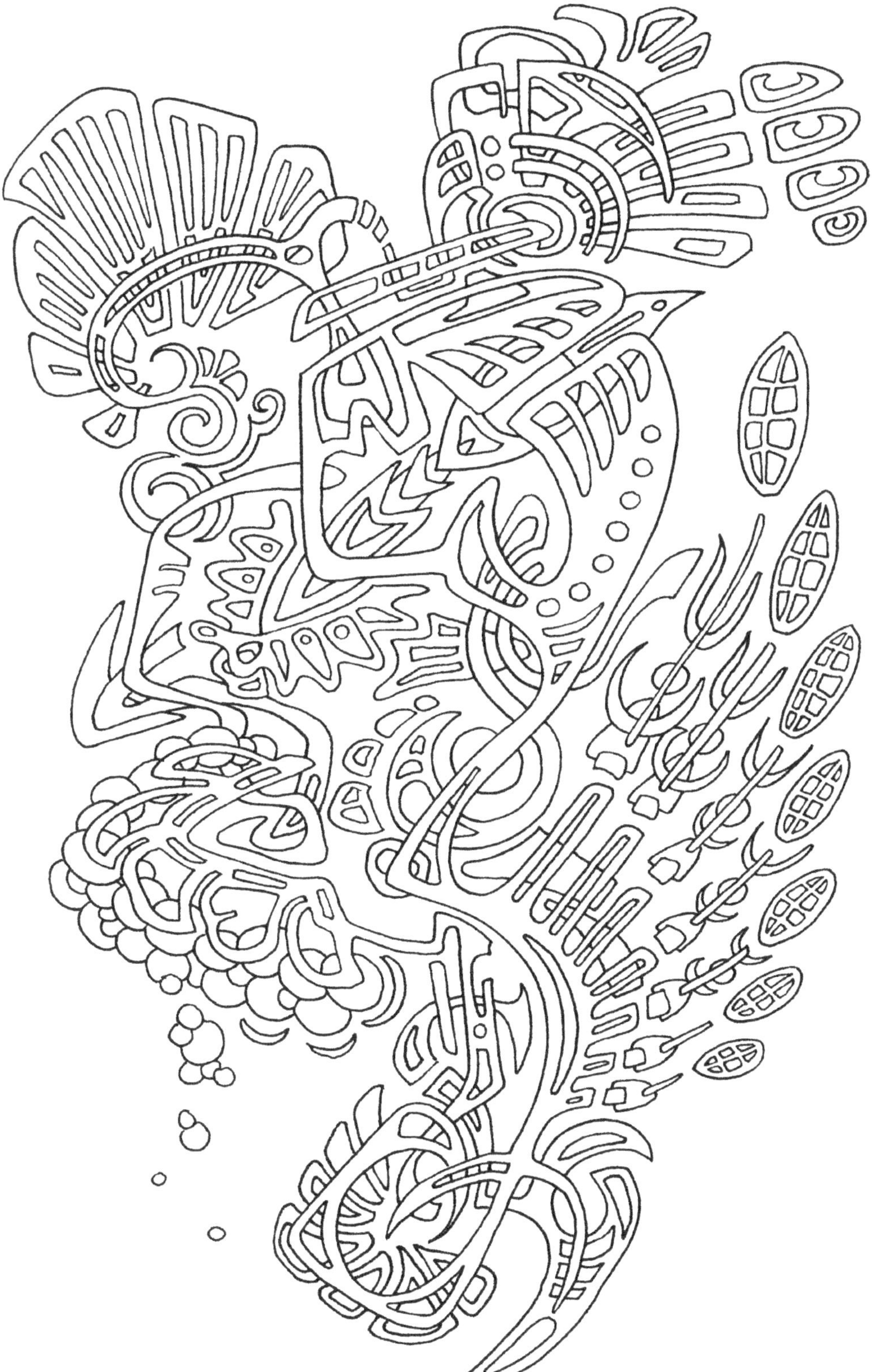

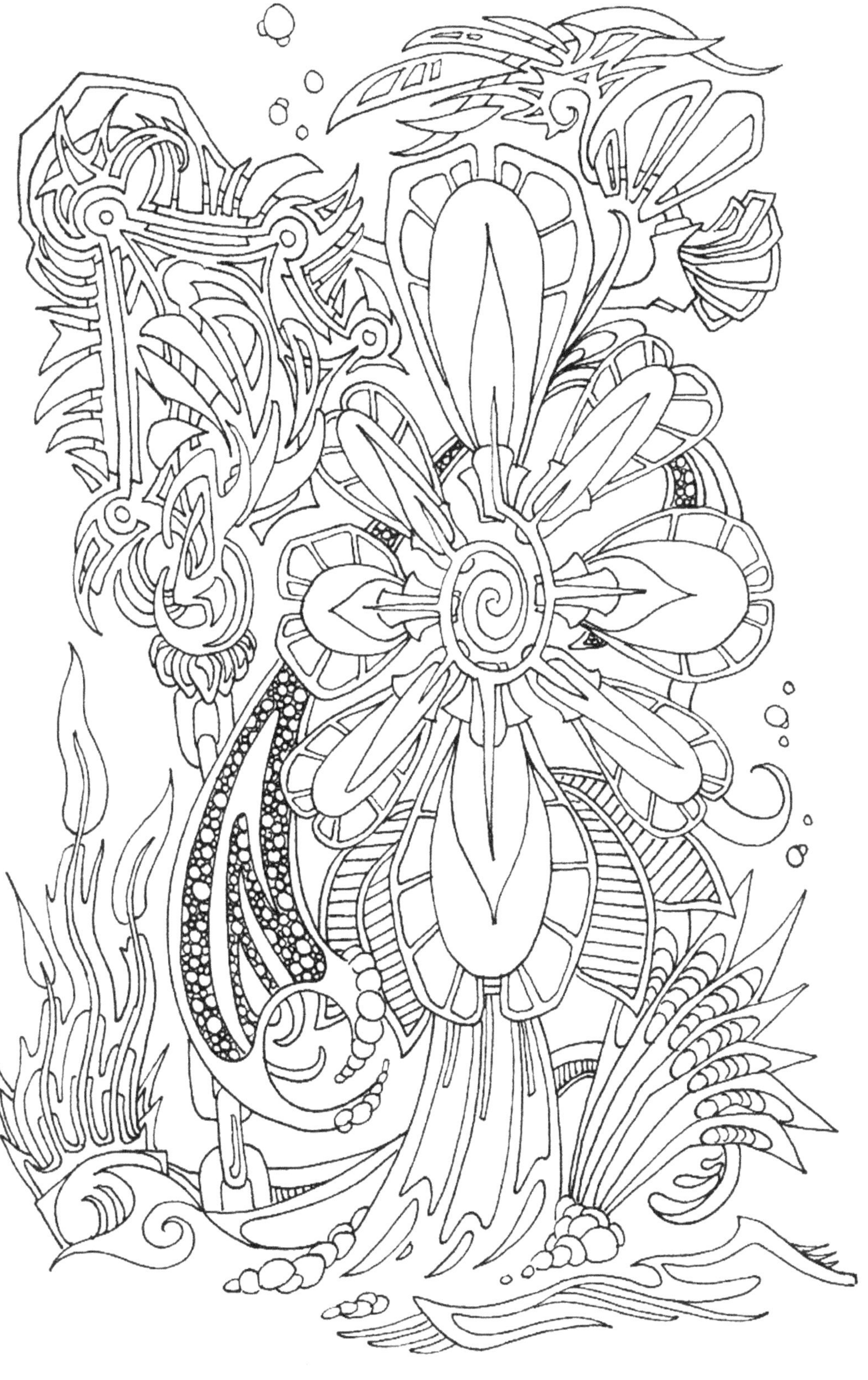

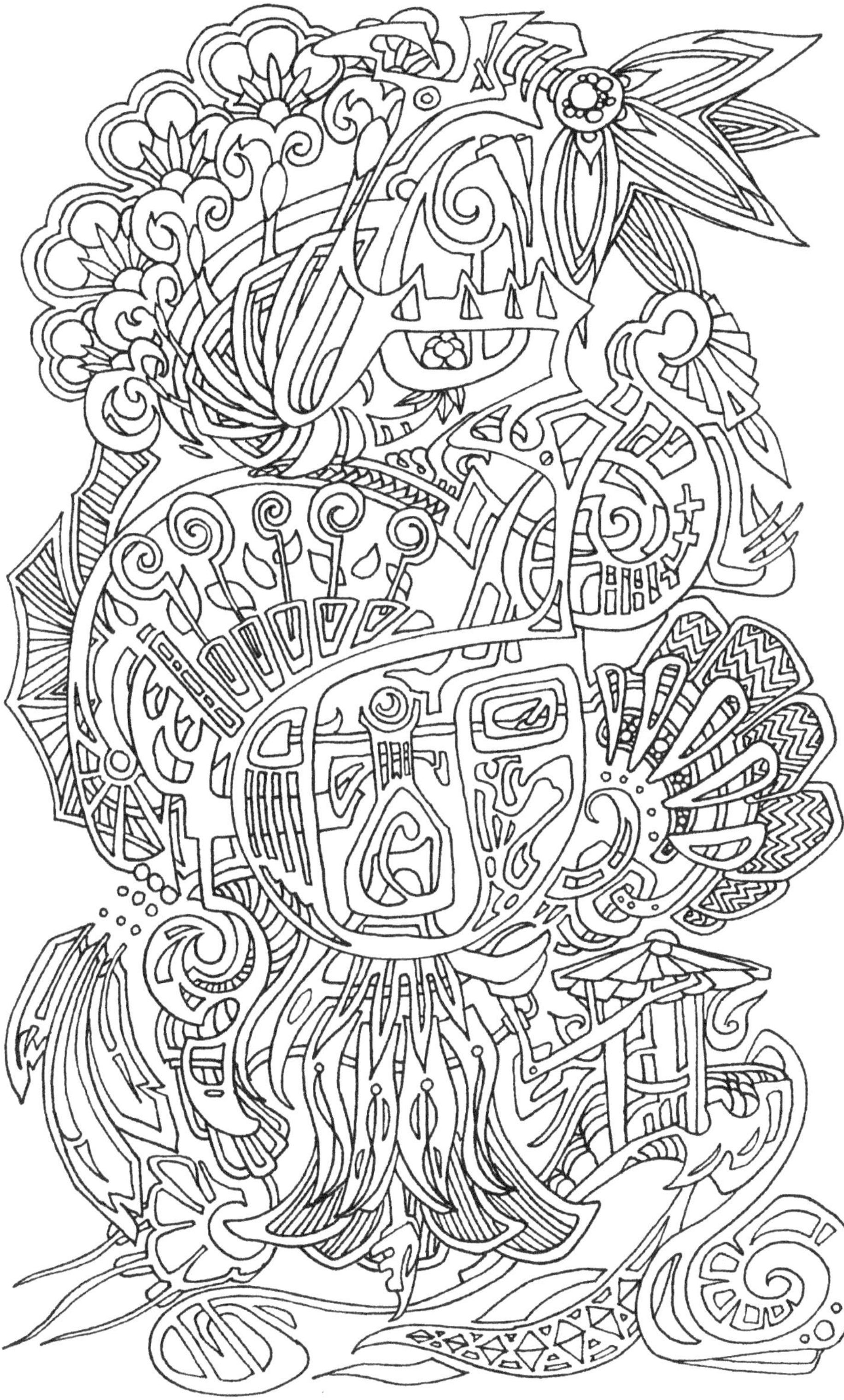

www.ingramcontent.com/pod-product-compliance
Lightning Source LLC
Chambersburg PA
CBHW071641170526
45166CB00003B/1385
* 9 7 8 1 5 2 2 7 0 2 8 9 4 *